D1371759

WILDCATS

Jaguars

by Jennifer L. Marks

Consulting Editor: Gail Saunders-Smith, PhD

Consultant: Robin Keith
Senior Research Coordinator
San Diego Zoo's Institute for Conservation Research

CAPSTONE PRESS
a capstone imprint

Pebble Plus is published by Capstone Press,
151 Good Counsel Drive, P.O. Box 669, Mankato, Minnesota 56002.
www.capstonepub.com

Books published by Capstone Press are manufactured with paper
containing at least 10 percent post-consumer waste.

Library of Congress Cataloging-in-Publication Data
Marks, Jennifer, 1979–
    Jaguars / by Jennifer L. Marks.
    p. cm.—(Pebble plus. Wildcats)
    Includes bibliographical references and index.
    Summary: "Simple text and full-color photos explain the habitat, life cycle, range, and behavior of jaguars"—
Provided by publisher.
    ISBN 978-1-4296-4481-5 (library binding)
    1. Jaguar—Juvenile literature. I. Title. II. Series.
QL737.C23M2746 2011
599.75'5—dc22   2010002798

Editorial Credits
Katy Kudela, editor; Bobbie Nuytten, designer; Svetlana Zhurkin, media researcher; Eric Manske, production specialist

Photo Credits
Ardea/Nick Gordon, 17
Corbis/W. Perry Conway, cover
Creatas, 9
Dreamstime/John Anderson, 5
Getty Images/Discovery Channel Images/Jeff Foott, 14–15
McDonald Wildlife Photography/Joe McDonald, 12–13
Minden Pictures/Michael & Patricia Fogden, 21
Peter Arnold/BIOS, 7; Gerard Lacz, 18–19
Shutterstock/ecoventurestravel, back cover, 11; Ewan Chesser, 1; Fenton (paw prints), cover and throughout

The author dedicates this book to Bethy Twaddle and her friend Nosara, a jaguar at La Marina Wildlife Rescue Center
    in Costa Rica.

Note to Parents and Teachers

The Wildcats series supports national science standards related to life science. This book
describes and illustrates jaguars. The images support early readers in understanding the
text. The repetition of words and phrases helps early readers learn new words. This book
also introduces early readers to subject-specific vocabulary words, which are defined in the
Glossary section. Early readers may need assistance to read some words and to use the Table of
Contents, Glossary, Read More, Internet Sites, and Index sections of the book.

Printed in the United States of America in North Mankato, Minnesota.
032011   006102R

Table of Contents

At Home in the Forest

Big yellow eyes peer

through jungle leaves.

It is a jaguar keeping cool

in the shade.

Jaguars live in Mexico and Central and South America. These large cats prowl rain forests, swamps, grasslands, and forests.

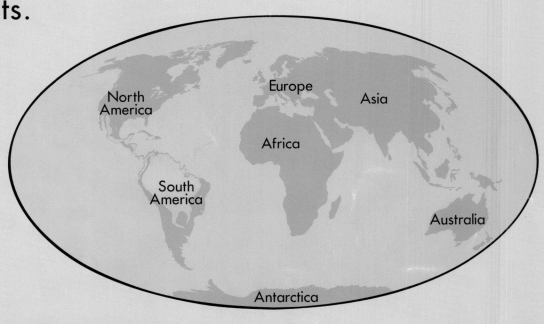

□ where jaguars live

Jaguar Bodies

Jaguars are the third-largest member of the cat family. These large cats can weigh up to 300 pounds (136 kilograms).

house cat

jaguar

Jaguars have thick coats
of tan or black fur.
Spots on their coats
help them stay hidden
in the shadows.

Jaguars use their short, powerful legs to climb trees. Their strong legs help them swim in rivers too.

On the Hunt

A hunting jaguar

creeps close to its prey.

Snap! The jaguar uses

its strong jaws and sharp

teeth to grab its prey.

Jaguars hunt on land,
in water, and in trees.
They eat capybaras, tapirs,
deer, caimans, and turtles.
Jaguars even catch fish.

Jaguar Life Cycle

Jaguars mate at
all times of the year.
Females give birth to
litters of up to four cubs.

As adults, jaguars live alone.
They rub and scratch trees
to mark their home range.
Jaguars live 12 to 15 years
in the wild.

Glossary

caiman—a Central and South American reptile that looks like a crocodile

capybara—a pig-sized rodent with partly webbed feet and no tail

cub—a young jaguar

litter—a group of animals born at the same time to one mother

mate—to join together to produce young

prey—an animal hunted by another animal for food

prowl—to move around quietly and secretly

range—an area where an animal naturally lives

tapir—a large, piglike animal that has hooves and a long nose

Read More

Murray, Julie. *Jaguars*. Animal Kingdom. Edina, Minn.: Abdo Pub., 2005.

Pitts, Zachary. *The Pebble First Guide to Wildcats*. Pebble First Guides. Mankato, Minn.: Capstone Press, 2009.

Internet Sites

FactHound offers a safe, fun way to find Internet sites related to this book. All of the sites on FactHound have been researched by our staff.

Here's all you do:

Visit *www.facthound.com*

FactHound will fetch the best sites for you!

Index

Word Count: 178

Grade: 1

Early-Intervention Level: 17